MORE OF
MILTON KEYNES

ROBERT COOK

SUTTON PUBLISHING

Sutton Publishing Limited
Phoenix Mill · Thrupp · Stroud
Gloucestershire · GL5 2BU

First published 2004

Title page: Although this is a recent picture
of All Saints' Church in Milton Keynes little
has changed from photographs taken a
century ago, apart from the clothing of
these people discussing church affairs, and
the lamp post. *(Robert Cook)*

British Library Cataloguing in Publication Data
A catalogue record for this book is available from the
British Library.

ISBN 0-7509-3859-5

Typeset in 10.5/13.5 Photina.
Typesetting and origination by
Sutton Publishing Limited.
Printed and bound in England by
J.H. Haynes & Co. Ltd, Sparkford.

Bletchley ladies take a break from making Rodex coats, *c.* 1955. *(Pam Essam)*

CONTENTS

Rush hour at Milton Keynes Central, where trains are often late and commuters must hurry, September 2003. (*Robert Cook*)

INTRODUCTION

When the Revd Mr Bromley of the parishes of Broughton and Milton Keynes was informed that his neighbourhood was going to be engulfed by new city development, he commented: 'I don't think the town will affect me personally, but I hope to have larger congregations.' There was a man who knew what life was all about – doing business. In the country that started the industrial revolution, it is surprising that by the 1960s antagonism between workers and bosses had become a culture of 'us and them'. Milton Keynes might be seen in some sense as an effort by Harold Wilson's Labour government to move beyond this impasse in order to unlock some of the nation's potential. The continued existence of class rhetoric about rich ghettos and nimbys suggests, however, that some things have not changed.

The Labour Party was founded on idealism and the Conservative on the need to make a profit. Prophets and profits are uncomfortable bedfellows but both parties agreed to push ahead with what has become known as the new city of Milton Keynes, even though, for financial reasons, it has never officially been given that status.

Now that the original 30-year plan approaches maturity, Milton Keynes finds itself back in the news. Apparently the town's amazing success has led the government to choose it as the focus for a new centre of population growth, though centre is not exactly the right word, since most of the growth pushes at the boundaries of rural north Buckinghamshire so impacted by the original settlement. There is inevitable unrest in the countryside. Town planner David Lock of David Lock Associates, who are involved with the expansion plan, said: 'The eighteen communities involved in the plan have their destinies interwoven with the new city. Instead of facing up to doing a deal with the enquiry panel [for the Milton Keynes and South Midlands Sub-Regional Strategy] they are still at the very primitive tribal stage with the typical view of rural Tories looking down their noses at the rough urbanites. But if an 18-foot fence went up around the city they would be the first to be inconvenienced. Which way do they think the traffic flows?'

This brief study opens with a few images and words about the 'good old days'. But pretty pictures can hide a world of squalor, and work was hard. The local rich had perhaps made good but people of substance could trace their origins back to the Norman invaders and perhaps even Saxon overlords. Self-made folk of recent vintage can appear jumped-up or vulgar, but the old ruling classes of the Duke of Buckingham variety could be arrogant, cruel and ruthless, happy to see the lower orders slave or work for a pittance, starve and fight wars for them.

Although high-handed behaviour from old and new money can still be witnessed, the real problem is that we have advanced enough to want to give everyone a chance in life but – short of utopian communism or a 'brave new world' – you can't make everyone equal. There is little room in Fullers Slade for vigorous young boys to flex muscles or spread wings. Some years ago Bletchley's idealistic newspaper editor Ron Staniford chastised me for writing that the Lakes estate in Bletchley had problems because it had been a dumping ground for London's problem families. He said there was good in everybody. This outlook does not seem to be shared by his successors at the *Milton Keynes Gazette*, who vilify the town's sex offenders and women beaters. And there are all too many other crimes and a maximum security prison to go with these, but there are not enough policemen. One police source told me that the town was built for crime – the estates are ideal and social deprivation fuels it. A teacher said there are levels of social deprivation affecting children in Milton Keynes that are on a par with and often worse than those found in our most run-down inner cities.

Bad housing is one factor bound to have an impact on family life but, for all the grand plans to build more, prices continue to rise beyond the reach of many people. The government estimates that 120,000 new homes need to be built annually over and above current proposals in order to have any effect on national property price inflation. Council leader Liberal Isobel Wilson has taken issue with the government over their expansion plans, demanding that funding be made available for provision of the infrastructure required by new housing because it was not fair to ask existing residents to pay. The response was silence. Then Brian White MP, former Labour deputy leader of the town's first unitary authority, said in December 2003 that Milton Keynes had managed in his time on £100 million less than his government was giving the town. In March 2004 we were informed that the town's internal auditors had criticised the lack of effective financial systems and controls within the council. Overspends were attributed to a poor culture of budgetary responsibility and accountability rather than individual officers' misconduct. In the current financial year the Liberal Democrat council has overspent by £1.2 million, including £679,000 on children's social services. The report had been kept secret since last November.

Life is never that simple, however. The council has been taking on more and more services and the cost of meeting the city's spending priorities is constantly being loaded on to the council – and Milton Keynes Council has to take the blame for a government that does not want to give them enough money to manage the proposed rapid growth.

These are challenging times – of family breakdown, asylum seekers and economic migrants. Even if national government takes some of the burden, the sum total of incomers affects the town in subtle ways. All that overspend went on something more than councillors' extra expenses, and many needs are being ignored, regardless of all the rhetoric about economic growth. Drug problems and suicide rates are a further misery of city life, and hasty provision of more housing will not alleviate these problems whatever the spin-doctors may say.

A further problem is that Milton Keynes lacks a good public transport system. Consequently people who cannot afford to buy a house must still commit themselves to expenditure on a car. This is not what Lord Campbell of Eskan and his Development Corporation intended back in the 1960s, when some good planning led to many of the town's potential strengths – which should be built upon, not swamped. Milton Keynes could and should be a true garden city, not 'Pack-'em-in-cheapville'. James Buxton, an urban planner in the 1970s who helped design parts of the city, wants to use some of the ideas back in his Ghanaian home-town, Nyanyaano. He said they need a mini-Milton Keynes where thought has gone into infrastructure.

A lot of thought may have gone into infrastructure, but the town had to wait until the late 1970s before gaining a hospital with an A&E department that could handle 16,500 patients a year – and it actually has to deal with 65,000. Some argue that not enough thought is going into new infrastructure and that it will be provided on an ad hoc basis, after building houses and then playing catch up. When the new development ball started rolling back in 2001 they were talking of building on parking spaces, adding multi-storey car parks on the city's edge, to be served by better public transport, aiming to create an environment which attracts value jobs.

In spite of losing de Montfort University, the Open University (the world's largest university with 150,000 students worldwide) has thrived because Milton Keynes is central and there are no students to accommodate and entertain on site. But the enquiry will be considering the issue of creating a university and a teaching hospital here. This might help gloss over the fact that the skills base of the local economy is not strong. But what is the point of a university? Are the government not listening to Professor Steven Schwartz, the chair of their enquiry into university admissions, who wants the abolition of a funding system that guarantees all institutions enough students but stops the best from expanding? The proposals for a new university appear to be an irrelevant piece of window-dressing, albeit one that provides insight into this strange expansion process! In an age of educational inflation and potentially falling demand, a university hardly seems a priority.

At least the report recognised the need for fundamental access to education and information opportunities. For all the talk of civic pride, many feel excluded in a corporate environment dominated by the weakness of our times, image and gloss. While this may make the chattering classes feel good about themselves, smugness is no way to real progress. Local lorry driver and artist Bill Billings made the point, in an early 1970s TV documentary, saying that a particular type of person was coming into town and taking over. But if such a group monopolises Milton Keynes they will use all their resources to stifle criticism and create a stale environment that no amount of trendy sculpture or bourgeois artwork can ameliorate. I think this is a real danger and wish to challenge that outlook.

The town centre already has something of a cultural reputation, though there were some sniggers when it was mooted that the bus depot and stations should be sold to pay for the new theatre and art gallery. It depends how closely one holds to the view that Milton Keynes was founded as a proletarian paradise rather than as a bastion for the bourgeoisie. However, there are plans to develop and diversify the cultural scene. Consultants EDAW said that most people wanted the shopping centre to be more than a place to shop.

As the land between Snelshall and Tattenhoe Street is filled in and houses spew into Buckinghamshire along the road from the Bottle Dump roundabout to Newton Longville, we can see the 1960s dream coming to an end with much of its promise unfulfilled. And then we move into the unknown. Land value will multiply by 300 according to Treasury figures, and if developers pay a handsome tax they need not build to meet the needs of first-time buyers. With so many desperate for their own place and Prescott's new high-density proposals for green-field sites, new houses may indeed be little more than 'sentry boxes'. Retired Bletchley bank manager Alan Taylor says: 'Everything has changed since I came here in 1966. . . . But it would be wrong to say that Milton Keynes has been a failure. . . . I live in Nash, a pleasant village. If Milton Keynes were to swallow us up it would destroy our community. We came here for the views. . . . At the same time we accept that Milton Keynes will grow if a lot of big money has gone into it. The government want it, but if you live in an area of great beauty you are not just going to let it happen.'

So when nimbys shout, it still might be worth listening. Is it a crime to want to preserve the countryside and diversity? Can't Milton Keynesians have a home and countryside as once intended? Must their city be expanded for newcomers when Birmingham and Coventry are saying, 'Send it here, help us regenerate brown-field sites'? Are the government fools or are there things they are not telling us? Why has government used a process so undemocratic, consulting only who they want to? As Buckinghamshire County Council Chairman Richard Pushman told the CPRE's AGM at Longueville Hall: 'Mr Prescott does not seem to follow the normal pattern of political consultation.' Indeed not, and so we may look forward to 'More Milton Keynes'.

Robert Cook, May 2004

1

BC – Before Concrete

Staple Hall entrance, Fenny Stratford, *c.* 1916. Milton Keynes was a village among meadows with the Ouzel river, fed by little brooks and streams, slowly draining the land, a land where all was slow, governed by the seasons and rigid social hierarchy. There was quiet suffering from poverty and limited health care. In the last analysis, those with big money had the final word, as they do today. Milton Keynes once looked idyllic, but pretty thatched cottages could be hovels. The growing towns of Bletchley and Wolverton attracted folk from near and far, from declining agriculture at the turn of the nineteenth century, mainly into the railway trades and the Fletton brick industry. Two world wars upset the old order. New industries and opportunities raised new hopes for common people. Milton Keynes was perhaps the biggest hope north Buckinghamshire ever had, though the first plans made no connection with the village of Milton Keynes. That village had historic connections with the family of economist John Maynard Keynes and his namesake city was and still is very much an economic experiment. Built around the two old railway towns, infilling and reaching out to the original little village, Milton Keynes has a name that once sounded warm, but related to the vastness of the new city's estates and commerce it may now seem cold and clinical. *(Author's collection)*

Watling Street, Old Stratford, *c. 1920.* This is the way to Northampton and Buckingham. Horses and carts would prevail for years to come and the journey around what are now the new city limits was long and winding, each occasional village in a world of its own. *(Author's collection)*

The approach to Wolverton from Stony Stratford, *c. 1906.* The scene here is nowadays much changed: it was decorous to be well-dressed, whether young or old, and not just for the camera. External image was everything. *(Author's collection)*

The Green, in the market town of Stony Stratford, *c.* 1910. As we shall see later in the book, the Green is still very recognisable from this picture, but motor cars abound. The Roman Watling Street lies in the distance at the end of this road and has been much used over the centuries by rulers of the land. Richard III stole nephew Prince Edward away from the town, to murder and rid himself of a rival, such was the routine brutality of the ruling classes. *(Author's collection)*

John Wesley's Tree, Stony Stratford, *c.* 1910. Two fires destroyed much of the old town and then came Milton Keynes: old trees were felled and new ones planted. Elms were doomed long before, with the terrible Dutch Elm disease. This picture was taken when the tree under which John Wesley preached still stood. Not far away a house carried the inscription 'Time and Fire destroy all things'. *(Author's collection)*

The Tram Terminus, Stony Stratford, early 1900s. This was a busy interchange, used, as we can see, by the more versatile and ultimately predominant motor buses. The Wolverton and Stony Stratford Tramways Co. was formed in November 1882, working mainly as transport for Wolverton Railway works operatives. Although 1*s* a day was a lot out of 25*s* a week, it was quicker and easier than walking and services reached Deanshanger. *(Author's collection)*

The McCorquodales' limousine, *c.* 1918, at their home Winslow Hall, where they were sometimes hosts to royalty, who occasionally rode with the Whaddon Chase during the 1920s. The wealthy could be kind to their underlings but the class system was rigid until the demands of war forced the aristocracy to allow a little more social mobility. The inter-war years saw the region thronged with ex-servicemen tramping streets and byways. The Jarrow marchers passed through and workhouses struggled to cope. Fears of revolution were quenched by the Hitler menace, and the lack of fit skilled persons to fight prompted thoughts of better education and a welfare state. The rich would have to adapt. *(Chris Phillips)*

Opposite, above: The High Street, Stony Stratford, *c.* 1907. Two grand old inns, the Cock and the Bull, are reckoned to give us the origin of the phrase 'cock-and-bull' stories, which derives apparently from stagecoach travellers passing time by telling far-fetched tales while supping ale during their stay in the hostelries. The Cock is renowned for many things, including a magnificent wooden carved doorway. It still hears many a tall story, especially during the weekly folk club, led by veteran Matt Armour. *(Author's collection)*

Opposite, below: Stratford Road, Wolverton, *c.* 1930. The little village of Wolverton grew rapidly in the late nineteenth century, with the engine and carriage works offering workers a range of opportunities, including diverse and better-paid skilled jobs. The rows of almost identical housing were aligned in the typical straight lines of those industrialising times. Stratford Road was the main route through town, close to the rail and printing works. The latter was the province of the wealthy McCorquodales, who lived in Winslow. The family name still appears on credit cards, though modernisation has seen the demise of local printing. Labour relations were not always harmonious and these streets have been thronged with striking printers. *(Author's collection)*

The Front, Wolverton, 1920s. The shops will soon be busy, deliveries are underway and a bus has probably dropped off the students for the local commercial college. Wolverton was a model town, on a busy railway line and on the Northamptonshire frontier. Telegraph poles appear very tall in an age where the phone is still a luxury. *(Author's collection)*

The church, New Bradwell, *c.* 1920. Bradwell had an abbey in the twelfth century and is a very old place of similar age. New Bradwell was a nineteenth-century extension for railway workers but the little church does not lack beauty. The Church gave comfort and joy to all those who suffered and working people suffered more than most – wars claimed family and so did the many diseases and occupational accidents of those good old days. *(Author's collection)*

A favourite walk, Stantonbury, *c.* 1910. On the back of this postcard the message reads: 'Dear Avis, Would you like to come for a walk with me along the water side? Yours, Dad.' What more can one say, reading of such simple pleasures. Perhaps for all the hardships it was easier to be happy then! *(Author's collection)*

Corner Pin, Stantonbury, *c.* 1910. The name is now most associated with the large Stantonbury Comprehensive campus, and this once remote little place by the Ouse, dominated by a fine Norman church, has no such charm about it now. This picture is so very quaint, but Stantonbury had already lost vitality to Wolverton, the growing railway town. *(Author's collection)*

Bradwell station, viewed through the bridge, 27 August 1954, where the engine nicknamed 'Nobby Newport' once pulled the railway workers' trains back and forth between Newport Pagnell, Wolverton and Bletchley until the wicked Tory cuts reduced railways to a rump and promoted the egotism and environmental horrors and carnage of the car age. *(K. Barrow)*

Bradwell station remains, early 1980s. What's left of the old station still looks pretty, though pretty depressing to us train buffs! *(Colin Stacey)*

Canal bank, Newport Pagnell. The town stands on ground that rises from the south bank of the Ouse, which is crossed by a fine five-arched stone bridge and is joined by the River Lovatt after its trickle through the town. This image from 1906 reminds one of its glory days. Much longer ago there was a priory, founded in the days of William Rufus. *(Author's collection)*

Opposite: St John Street, Newport Pagnell. There's plenty of history in this town upon a high bank of the Ouse, garrisoned by Civil War royalists and harassed by Cromwell's men, though Cromwell lost a son here to smallpox in 1644. Here the town with its seventeenth- and eighteenth-century houses looks quaint in the fussy 1950s. Two ladies have time to talk. All is somewhat faster now, though in spite of Milton Keynes reaching out this far to claim the town Newport has not succumbed. *(Author's collection)*

The Swan Inn, Newport Pagnell, *c.* 1920. Newport has a long history of stage and bus travel. Here is an evocative image from the pioneering days. This would be the location of one of the legends of local bus travel, Bluebell Coaches, and later Wesley Brothers. *(Andrew Shouler)*

Market Square, Newport Pagnell, 11 May 1972. As the years passed and the National Bus Company evolved, the town was put on the Cheltenham–Yarmouth express service. Since deregulation many services have been down-graded and coach travellers are often poorly served. This picture shows the 182 United Counties service, as well as an excellent view of the old town. (Andrew Shouler)

Opposite, above: River Ouse, near Lavendon Mill, c. 1906. At this point we are moving away from Milton Keynes and the new city area, but expansion plans will bring traffic, noise and light pollution, encouraging development and more house price pressure from the better off. That all seems unimaginably far off in this old view of a place that contained ancient monuments long before William the Conqueror's arrival and that was once the home of Sir Isaac Newton's ancestors. (Author's collection)

Opposite, below: Cowper's summerhouse, Olney, Buckinghamshire. Again, this is just beyond the scope of the new city but not beyond its massive influence. The proximity of the M1 in the east has been used to counter expansion eastward, much to the annoyance of many in the west! This is the poet Cowper's summerhouse, the church spire peeping over the hedge, looking like the hat of a giant witch in this old image. Living nineteen years in Olney, the troubled poet would often have agonised inside the confines of this little cabin. What interesting thoughts he must have had. Perhaps, like me writing this, he was completely oblivious of his surroundings and inconsiderate of those around him. Writing is such a selfish pastime. (Author's collection)

Clifton Bridge, Olney, *c.* 1905. All this water, like so much of life, has passed through the region we now call Milton Keynes. How long before the expanding city claims this and more? There are those who say this is a region of no great beauty but this picture tells another story. Having said that, much land has long been claimed by the powerful and there is the view that with enough thought, planning and money such beauty could be enhanced and we could have a city of great parks open to all, not just the rich. *(Author's collection)*

Opposite: Olney Church, late 1940s. It has been said that Olney without Cowper would have only this church, with its sturdy great stone spire, and two curates to boast of. The church is fourteenth century with a pinnacled tower. *(Author's collection)*

Swan Hotel, Woburn Sands, *c*. 1908. Another view of Woburn, from the Duke of Bedford's land, so close to Milton Keynes yet so far away. The Enquiry in Public Panel has heard that plans to develop Bedford are simply easing the way to provide housing already under consideration, and are about freeing up the system. Britain is already the most built-up country in Europe, its people on average paying the most for the smallest housing, which is increasingly concentrated around areas like Milton Keynes. It is a moot point as to whether this is as sustainable an approach to development as Mr Prescott argues or that it would fulfil European criteria. *(Author's collection)*

Opposite, above: Great Brickhill village, early 1950s. Milton Keynes town planner David Lock said: 'There is very little opposition to the eastern expansion of Milton Keynes because it affects very few people. There's anxiety expressed by people in Bow Brickhill and maybe a handful in Broughton. Half of the new plan is proposed in the local plan anyway.' Great Brickhill is closer to the action, with the Stoke Hammond bypass and Newton Leys estate, but the village, which sits on sandhills looking into Bedfordshire, is still attractive in spite of so many more cars, with its thirteenth-century church and old cottages. *(Ken Barrow)*

Opposite, below: Aspley Hill, Woburn Sands, *c*. 1910. Interested parties from neighbouring Bedfordshire have been invited to observe plans for Milton Keynes expansion because, as part of the rather vague Prescott plans, it is stated that neighbouring authorities will have to plan for effects of the second phase of Milton Keynes development. The scene shown here is inevitably changed, but there is still much worth preserving. Such locations are already affordable only to the few and government plans to offer interest-free loans of up to £100,000 will hardly help because those with more money will simply push up prices further. The problem lies with having no real alternative to the private housing market. *(Author's collection)*

Fuller's Earth Lodge, Woburn Sands. The name here sounds very reassuring. Earth is much preferable to the impenetrability of concrete. Nothing grows on concrete except mould. Milton Keynes aspires to be green yet so admires concrete that it is famous for concrete cows as a piece of art. Locals don't like jokes about such things, I am told. For some, Milton Keynes is a way of life, a belief even, but it is a place on earth and it is owed to us all that it be sustainable – let those in authority take note. *(Author's collection)*

Millbrook station, 11 September 1958. This station is just outside the Milton Keynes area yet might easily have been part of the expansion scheme had the M1 not acted as a barrier. Critics argue that this is no good reason because the land is more marginal and it would make sense to expand in the direction of the Bedford urban area. Whatever the case may be, it is a quaint little station and is still served by trains from Bletchley to Bedford. It is a mystery with so much of the old Oxbridge line being torn up that this section has survived. If it is possible here then why not give the rest a chance? Millbrook will inevitably feel the heat from planned Milton Keynes growth, which is why neighbouring authorities have been invited as observers to the enquiry. They will have to deal with the consequences and inevitable increased housing and transport needs. *(Ken Barrow)*

Grand Union Canal, Simpson lock, early 1900s. The lock-keeper's house is far right. It was here, during the First World War, that 52-year-old Edith Mary Scott, the lock-keeper's wife, fell off the open swingbridge the day after her 62-year-old husband William Henry died following a long illness. She was attempting to cross the bridge in the dark. The lock was a popular fishing venue. *(Colin Scott)*

A satisfied customer in the 1930s outside Billy Golding's shop, Aylesbury Street, Fenny Stratford. Mr Golding won prizes for his recipe but would not divulge it to Walls despite being offered a fortune for it. *(Colin Scott)*

The Three Trees pub, Buckingham Road, Bletchley, *c.* 1900. The pub was a favourite until the 1960s when new city ways took over and it was demolished. *(Pam Essam)*

Drayton Road allotments, Bletchley, *c.* 1950. Every railwayman grew his own vegetables back then, and some still do, but Milton Keynes is a good place for shopping. *(Eddy Hancock)*

A rear garden in Middlesex Drive, Bletchley. The 1960s saw its first big influx of newcomers, though some Londoners like my late father came as long ago as the 1950s. Housing was scarce. *(P.J. Stanley)*

The garden at 110 Whaddon Way, *c.* 1960. In those early days there were miles of countryside and real freedom for newcomers to Bletchley. What a pity those joys couldn't last for ever. *(P.J. Stanley)*

The *City of Liverpool*, on shed after failing at Bletchley and having repairs, early 1950s. After a period of being steadily run down, Bletchley motive power depot is earmarked for closure. *(K.J.C. Jackson)*

There have been no significant repair facilities at Bletchley since the demise of steam and British Railways. Here we see an English, Welsh and Scottish railways mobile workshop making repairs to a failed Virgin loco in May 2003. Sir Richard Branson's company name inevitably gives the impression of someone who likes breaking new ground, nomenclature most apt for the unfolding saga of Milton Keynes. *(Robert Cook)*

The Micheline – the first train on pneumatic tyres, in commercial use from 1931 – shown during trials on the LMS Bletchley–Oxford line. The straightness of the route from Bletchley to Verney Junction made it an ideal testbed for this pioneering design. Postwar diesel railcars proved very economical in sustaining the Oxford–Cambridge and Oxford–Banbury routes, but a government hell-bent on a motorway future closed the line in 1967. Today's new town expanders face the consequences of trying to pack more traffic on overloaded roads or find ways of reinstating the line, which has been built over beyond Bedford. *(Colin Scott)*

Home of the royal train and fine craftsmanship, this is Wolverton Railway Works in the early 1980s, before Tory policies ate into British Rail. The author recalls debating the future of the royal train on BBC Radio Solent's Peter White show. According to a leading Tory the train is not extravagantly furnished; much of it involves Formica. So when I was asked to what uses the train might be put between royal trips, I suggested a mobile DIY exhibition. Unfortunately we do very little manufacturing and Wolverton works is a shadow of its former self. *(Eddy Hancock)*

Children, parents and staff at Newton Longville School, 2 miles south of Bletchley, early 1950s. Newton Longville was named after a Benedictine monastery in Normandy when Walter Giffard established a cell here in the twelfth century. *(Midge Day)*

Newton Longville School today. Having been reclaimed by the diocese when a new one opened, the old building served as a village hall until a development application. This was refused and the building has been gradually decaying. I am told that some youngsters use it for illicit drinking and worse. *(Robert Cook)*

The church of St Faith and its fifteenth-century spire, in Newton Longville. The building stands on a raised churchyard near the crossroads. As Arthur Mee wrote, 'it is big and impressive'. *(Robert Cook)*

The old Red Lion, opposite the church, has moved with the times and trends of sophisticated Milton Keynes. As we can see, it is now a Thai restaurant, next door to the Mane Attraction, a fashionable hairstylist. *(Robert Cook)*

Whaddon Road, near Newton Longville, looking east toward the village. Land on both sides of this road is earmarked for 2,500 houses. Some villagers are critical of Buckinghamshire and Aylesbury Vale Councils for neglecting their needs and are unhappy about plans that could place them eventually within Milton Keynes' new town boundaries. Villagers have complained about the existing water supply and the April expansion enquiry heard that the south-east has less water per head than Syria. Anglian Water said that expansion plans were outside their 25-year business plan but they viewed new demands as a challenge. Developers said that they should be allowed to proceed, disagreeing with Milton Keynes Council's spokesman, who said the plans were over-ambitious. Whaddon Road, which joins the A421 at Bottle Dump roundabout, could be relieved by a southern bypass extending from the Whaddon roundabout to Cowpasture Farm but the east–west rail link, which would cut between the old village and new housing, is not definite and there is no funding. Public transport currently accounts for 4 per cent of all local journeys, with 7,000 people exiting and entering Milton Keynes morning and night. Planners hope that improved stops, punitive parking charges and park-and-ride schemes will help quadruple this figure. A new district hospital may be built at Bottle Dump roundabout. *(Robert Cook)*

Calverton village, near Stony Stratford, threatened by various schemes to extend Milton Keynes over the Whaddon ridge and proof, if any were needed, that this is beautiful countryside. In this photograph, taken from the Milton Keynes boundary, we see evidence of the ubiquitous car. *(Robert Cook)*

STRATEGIC OVERVIEW OF THE WES

The issue of sustainability recurred frequently during the April 2004 enquiry. This question needs setting in context of whether the whole pattern of world economic development is sustainable. Britain is a country running to keep up with world economic growth which, to the author, appears to be based on cheap energy, third world exploitation, destructive agriculture, small expensive housing, consumer debt and overwork. As the nation's most dynamic economy, according to the government, Milton Keynes must take on an increased role in these processes. At least David Lock's plans shown here for a sustainable expansion attempt to recognise the need for Milton Keynes to maintain its spacious and green-oriented outlook, with due attention to public transport. *(David Lock Associates)*

Overleaf: Needs must when the devil drives! This is the Strategic Vision for Milton Keynes expansion, showing elements of compromise and economy necessitated by the government's brief. Proper funding for infrastructure is conspicuously lacking from expansion proposals, along with the absence of any defined 30-year plan. The result is a great deal of anxiety around the intended development area. *(David Lock Associates)*

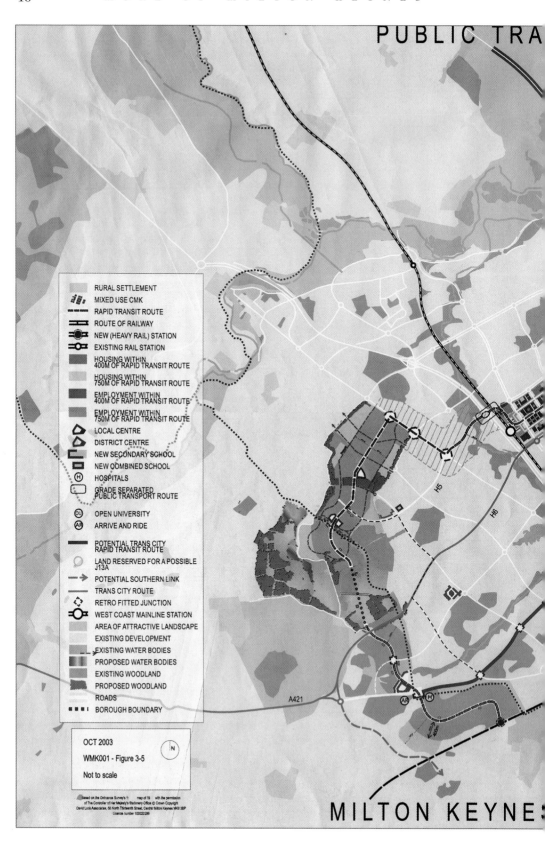

PUBLIC TRA

RURAL SETTLEMENT
MIXED USE CMK
RAPID TRANSIT ROUTE
ROUTE OF RAILWAY
NEW (HEAVY RAIL) STATION
EXISTING RAIL STATION
HOUSING WITHIN
400M OF RAPID TRANSIT ROUTE
HOUSING WITHIN
750M OF RAPID TRANSIT ROUTE
EMPLOYMENT WITHIN
400M OF RAPID TRANSIT ROUTE
EMPLOYMENT WITHIN
750M OF RAPID TRANSIT ROUTE
LOCAL CENTRE
DISTRICT CENTRE
NEW SECONDARY SCHOOL
NEW COMBINED SCHOOL
HOSPITALS
GRADE SEPARATED
PUBLIC TRANSPORT ROUTE
OPEN UNIVERSITY
ARRIVE AND RIDE
POTENTIAL TRANS CITY
RAPID TRANSIT ROUTE
LAND RESERVED FOR A POSSIBLE
J13A
POTENTIAL SOUTHERN LINK
TRANS CITY ROUTE
RETRO FITTED JUNCTION
WEST COAST MAINLINE STATION
AREA OF ATTRACTIVE LANDSCAPE
EXISTING DEVELOPMENT
EXISTING WATER BODIES
PROPOSED WATER BODIES
EXISTING WOODLAND
PROPOSED WOODLAND
ROADS
BOROUGH BOUNDARY

OCT 2003

WMK001 - Figure 3-5

Not to scale

Based on the Ordnance Survey's 1:   map of 59   with the permission
of The Controller of Her Majesty's Stationery Office © Crown Copyright
David Lock Associates, 50 North Thirteenth Street, Central Milton Keynes MK9 3BP
Licence number 100020299

A421

MILTON KEYNES

CORRIDORS

ATEGIC VISION

DAVID LOCK ASSOCIATES
TOWN PLANNING AND URBAN DESIGN

J 14

H5

M1 Motorway

H8

J 13

THE FOUNTAIN HOTEL, LOUGHTON, BUCKS.   "THE HOTEL WHICH IS DIFFERENT."

Images are deceptive, whether past or present. This one was no doubt idyllic for those who could afford to fly to the Fountain Hotel at Loughton, or travel in a grand limousine. Life was hard for the rural worker in the 1930s when this image was taken. The difference was they had space and the absence of hurry. We still have the longest working hours in Europe. There were pressures to conform, but were they any greater than those we have today? It is impossible to judge the standards of one generation by those of another, but we can wonder. *(Colin Scott)*

THE FOUNTAIN HOTEL

(Midway between Fenny Stratford and Stony Stratford
on the main London—Birmingham Road)

has it's own

PRIVATE AERODROME

1 mile S.S.W.

Pilots intending to land are requested to circle the Hotel three times and a car will meet them at the Aerodrome.

LONDON—47½ miles.
BIRMINGHAM—61 miles.

PROPRIETOR:
R. J. HARRISON,
LIEUT.-COMDR., R.N.

TEL.: SHENLEY-CHURCH-END 28.

Advertising material for the Fountain Hotel. *(Colin Scott)*

2

Doing It

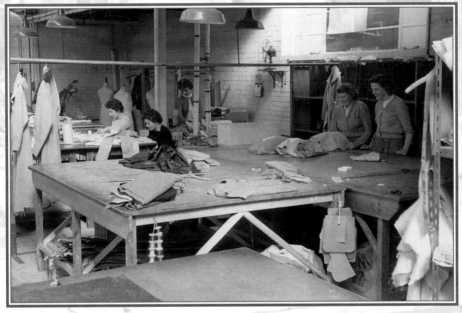

Local Tories and many farmers opposed the new city but nothing was going to stop Labour housing minister Richard Crossman, whose government had hijacked the original Buckinghamshire County Council proposals for a new town in north Buckinghamshire by refusing to fund a jobs programme to support the proposals. Prime Minister Harold Wilson was promising a white-hot technological revolution to modernise minds and British industry. In those days Bletchley had a manufacturing area along Watling Street in Fenny Stratford, as this picture shows with ladies hard at work in the little Rodex clothing factory where Harold's Gannex raincoats were made, among other things. Pam Essam, seated left, says, 'It was a happy place, with good social and sports facilities. We got on well with management.' Sadly such harmony was not commonplace and Labour had problems taming the unions that funded it. Before Milton Keynes was very far into development Mrs Thatcher was in power, dedicated to making unions obsolete, and with policies encouraging manufacturing to move abroad where labour was cheap. Milton Keynes was to have a future, along with the rest of the nation, in hi-tech knowledge-based industries and services where workers would have clean conditions and access to a consumer and leisure society. Scenes like this would become rare. *(Pam Essam)*

Posed for the camera at Newton Longville Brickyard, early 1960s. So great was the nationwide building boom that this local yard would not be able to meet demand for Milton Keynes house-building rates. Quickbuild Netherfield had to have other facings. *(Jack Bromfield)*

New house-building in Drayton Road, 1960s. The well-known Lakes Estate would soon take shape nearby, but meanwhile there was a great incentive toward in-filling like this example. Local housing shortages had been serious for many years. *(Eddy Hancock)*

Looking like a team of consultants from a *Carry On* film, the newly appointed Development Corporation gathers in the still peaceful village of Milton Keynes before it was engulfed and gave up its ancient name to a greater vision. Lord Campbell, third left, was not so impressed when he returned in the early 1990s, shortly before his death, and commented to the *Milton Keynes Citizen*, 'Look what they have done to my city.' Bradwell man, and chairman of Newport Pagnell Rural District Council, Ray Bellchambers, is far right. *(Wolverton Express)*

A map showing the designated new city development area. *(Ray Bellchambers)*

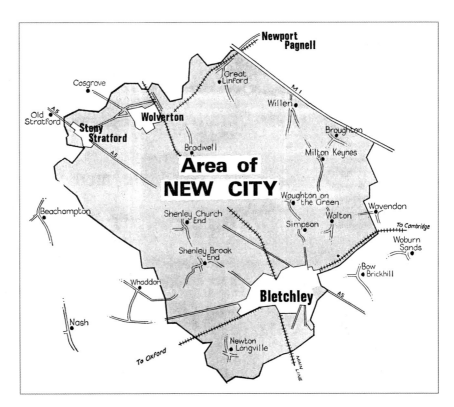

Every day was a quiet day on the M1 in its early years when this photograph was taken, near Newport Pagnell – at least by today's standards! The new city was chosen for several reasons, including proximity to this new motorway. The M1, planned by John Laing, was announced as 'the brightest ray of light yet in Britain's road picture', promising in 1958 to build the first 70 miles in 19 months, involving excavation of 11 million cubic yards of earth and laying 2,500 square yards of asphalt surface. There would be slip roads at Brogborough and Newport Pagnell. *(Reg Knapp)*

Lakes were going to be quite a feature of the new city. This is Beacon Lake, *c.* 1980, looking towards the Brickhills, a name redolent of the region's history in brick-making. *(Colin Stacey)*

Opposite, above: Caldecote Farm, seen here in the late 1980s, the last of the old farms in the central area, is soon to go. *(Colin Stacey)*

Opposite, below: Caldecote Farm in the late 1980s. The world of little ponds is fast disappearing, in this case making way for a new one of large lakes and water sports. *(Colin Stacey)*

Denbigh roundabout under construction. Grid roads and roundabouts were going to make the new city famous. The massive greenfield development involved in the project offered a clean slate to make straight criss-crossing carriageways. By the 1980s the moment had arrived to do the best possible to integrate the new system with the ways of Bletchley. *(Colin Stacey)*

Opposite, above: The old Roman Watling Street, through Fenny Stratford and north-east of old Bletchley, is being prepared for dual carriageways, in conjunction with roundabout improvements. The new roller-sports complex exemplifies the locality's increasing emphasis on leisure activity. *(Colin Stacey)*

Opposite, below: Shown here in the early 1980s, the new roundabout at the junction of Saxon Street (the B4034) and Watling Street looks abundantly green. *(Colin Stacey)*

Last days for a Bletchley landmark, the Rodex clothing factory, one of the town's first new industrial units along Watling Street. Closed for a while before this early 1980s picture was taken, it has been brightened up by the inevitable fly-poster brigade. *(Colin Stacey)*

It is sobering to see how easily the mightiest of buildings may be torn down. Against the force of modern machinery, the old Rodex factory soon crumbled into what we see here, opening up a view of the railway beyond. *(Colin Stacey)*

This Renault dealership, just south-east of Rodex, had not long been relocated from Whaddon Way; however, along with four neighbouring homes and Rodex, it would soon be demolished to accommodate a new Tesco superstore for the optimistic eighties. *(Colin Stacey)*

How are the mighty fallen! The site is cleared, and the increasing population of Milton Keynes will soon have another emporium! *(Colin Stacey)*

Milton Keynes may have been desperate for houses but they still had to be demolished if they were in the way of progress, like these two on the old A5 in Fenny Stratford. The sign says 'House clearance'. A.W. Mayles lived in the right-hand property. Perry's next door needed the land for an extended car lot. Milton Keynes was to be the city of the car driver. *(Colin Stacey)*

And so it came to pass that the car lot was cleared for more cheerful chariots. Soon these properties, including the old thatched farmhouse, would go too, making room for the Beacon Retail Park. 'Beacon' comes from the name of a local brush-maker, once situated nearby. *(Colin Stacey)*

Looking north towards Caldecote, across Simpson Road, 15 April 1983, from the roof of the Barclay printing offices. The Grand Union canal and the road give some welcome relief from the monotony of straight lines. Prime examples of 1970s and '80s cars line the car park. The groundwork for the new Bletcham Way Bridge can be seen clearly, just off centre-left. Being so close to Milton Keynes' eastern boundary and the River Ouzel, the area shows few signs of development to the right of the picture. *(Colin Stacey)*

Some time has passed since the previous scene, but little has changed except for more greenery and the new Bletcham Way Bridge linking Denbigh and Caldecote via the H10 grid road. *(Colin Stacey)*

Simpson and Woughton were among the first places to feel the heat of new city progress. Town centre development waited until well into the 1970s. Some of the housing around the centre has been criticised. One local gave a new meaning to residents being spaced out, speaking of a local drug problem. The council admitted they were unaware that some houses on Fishermead had been divided up for multiple occupation. Parish councillor Martin Petchley claimed a rash of bedsits was turning estates around the town into a ring of squalor. The author remembers working on Netherfield and being unaware of the dangers of materials like asbestos, so generously applied to Netherfield as a quick-build construction system. This image shows Mullion Place, Fishermead, looking north-east to the emerging new shopping centre building. *(Eddy Hancock)*

Milton Keynes is known as the city of trees and avenues, and this image shows the location in better light amid green abundance. There are concerns that government proposals to extend the limit on new large-scale developments to a minimum of 30 rather than 20 units an acre will undermine Milton Keynes' reputation as 'space city'. *(Eddy Hancock)*

Milton Keynes was conceived as a giant London overspill development, but the effects of the Thatcher era have changed all that, when local authorities were forced for ideological reasons to sell off properties, thus increasing demand pressures on house prices. Social housing is at a premium in the town and homes in the centre are very expensive. This view from a Fishermead bedroom would cost a fortune today. Here we see Xscape under construction, shortly before its opening in July 2000. *(Eddy Hancock)*

Xscape nears completion, looking something like a giant airship hangar. Figures revealed that four million people had used the facility in the first year, and there was a bumper celebration party that included live bands, giant penguins, huge cyborgs, skateboard demonstrations, BMX and Mad Mountain Bike displays. Its glamorous cinema facility has eclipsed the once glorious Point complex, which has now been taken over by the 'no frills' EasyJet boss to become a 'no frills' EasyCinema. The building is best known for indoor ski facilities and the re-frigeration unit makes the route past the back door very warm, even in winter. *(Eddy Hancock)*

There is currently planning permission for a third shopping centre extension around John Lewis's. This image shows the phase two extension under way in 1999. Milton Keynes has been criticised for its contribution to the nation's rampant consumerism. Edna Tunks suggests good reasons why folk might favour the place: 'It suits me being disabled, being as it's all flat. The big shops have got lifts and escalators. You haven't got to look where you put your feet all the time, not like in Bletchley. It's all on the flat. It's got everything I want. I don't know about other people. They've put extra disabled spaces in, so parking is no problem.' Her husband Des disagrees. 'I don't like it because it's all closed in and makes me feel dizzy.' But with education obsessed with getting everyone a selection of GCSEs and little time for life skills, the young are particularly vulnerable to the giant showcase of Milton Keynes shopping centre. Having the latest trendy stuff is the hallmark of success. It leads to such tragedies as that of Newport Pagnell teenager Aaron Trott whose debts led him to commit suicide in 2003. To update and expand Say's Law, 'Supply must create its own demand or there will be lots of job losses in service industry Britain.' *(Robert Cook)*

Opposite, above: Looking over the railway line and A5D from Child's Way, *c.* 1983. Winterhill Bus depot is clearly distinguished by large National Bus lettering on the bland side wall. This large facility brought together as strange bedfellows numerous cockney-rooted staff from Bletchley depot with the more rural minds of Stony Stratford in a cost-cutting exercise. Thatcher's hatchet years made sure the marriage didn't last. Privatisation eventually ended United Counties operations, making the depot unviable for its various successors. This too would be the fate of the British Rail livery carried by the passing Euston-bound express, and the neighbouring A5D would take on an even heavier load as traffic deserted the chaotic rail patchwork. *(Colin Stacey)*

Opposite, below: Viewed from almost the same spot in April 2000, a Virgin express is heading north; now much of the green space beyond the bus garage is infilled, with Chaffron Way bridge a gleaming crossing over road and rail, connecting with new development around Furzton and the Bowl. Winterhill bus depot was soon to be abandoned by Milton Keynes Metro and put up for development to help a cash-strapped council. *(Robert Cook)*

Childs Way under construction, seen from near Knowle Gate in the early 1980s, giving a clear view of the emergent rail and bus stations. I am informed that no expense was spared on the bus station and that the marble is real. Unfortunately, in car-mad Milton Keynes the bus station's relationship to people's needs was not, and it is little used – so much for integrated transport. *(Colin Stacey)*

Today the scene has matured; the middle distance is full of development and there are pavements in place that lead to nearby homes and workplaces. *(Robert Cook)*

Looking back towards Winterhill and the railway station from the bridge of Chaffron, early 1980s. *(Colin Stacey)*

The same location today: the road is busier and trees and gantries hide considerably increased development. Central reservation crash barriers are also in place as roads have become increasingly dangerous. *(Robert Cook)*

Part of Childs Way earthworks, early 1980s. *(Colin Stacey)*

A still idyllic view showing Loughton stables, a glimpse of a rural church and the new railway station from Childs Way, early 1980s. *(Colin Stacey)*

This is a pretty springtime scene of Loughton in 1983, and only a corner of the great railway station building reminds us of the presence of a growing town round and about. The picture was taken from the A5. *(Colin Stacey)*

A view from almost the same location, March 2004. It shows the old village housing alongside the A5 where so much of the new town development naturally took place, effectively filling in all the real space between Bletchley and Stony Stratford. *(Robert Cook)*

Grafton Street is a major thoroughfare (V6) extending from Watling Street (V4), north-east through the town centre to Grafton Gate. Here we see the new route emergent in all its glory, early in the 1980s. *(Colin Stacey)*

Opposite, above: To become part of Milton Keynes Loughton would have to have its roundabout and here it is, seen from the Bletchley side of the A5 in 1983 when there was still considerable open countryside. *(Colin Stacey)*

Opposite, below: Looking along the A5 from the same spot today the extent of local development is partly visible, but the signs directing people to new homes and also considerable service industry development are out of view. Great Holm fire station shows us exactly where we are in this ever-expanding town. *(Robert Cook)*

Old country roads like the A421 (still a B-road in the 1960s) had to find a new way through the dramatically altering landscape and so Milton Keynes became a place of many bridges as well as roundabouts. Under its new town name, Standing Way, we see the road diverted across this new bridge at Elfield Park looking towards Denbigh Hall. Watling Street (the old A5) lies straight ahead, and the new A5D runs below the bridge. *(Colin Stacey)*

A clear view of the A5D bridge carrying Standing Way across the virginal A5D in 1983. *(Colin Stacey)*

Rooksley, where major groundwork operations are in progress, as site markings indicate. The Ouse is sluggish, a fact noted in early surveys. Miles of concrete drainage pipes and manhole rings are necessary, a fact I know well as a former Milton Keynes pipelayer with Sidney Green's at Woughton on the Green in the early 1970s. *(Colin Stacey)*

This is the Thatcher age and British manufacturing is to be leaner and fitter – a euphemism for union-bashing and globalised companies shifting manufacturing to cheap-labour third-world economies. In time Britain's service economy would develop a similar appetite for cheap labour, to the extent that the British would end up occupying the smallest and most expensive houses in Western Europe, and many locals would soon experience deprivation levels on a par with the most run-down British inner-city areas. Meantime, British systems building proceeds apace and, as we can see here, a major new construction is completed at Rooksley within the year. More new jobs would arrive in the predominantly service economy of Milton Keynes. *(Colin Stacey)*

Great Holm, near Two Mile Ash and Kiln Farm, off Watling Street, *c.* 1980. Closely packed but substantial housing lines the horizon. This is a quality neighbourhood in a place of extremes. Foundations mark the site of more to come. Arthur Lyttle, working for the Development Corporation, said, 'There was some social engineering at the outset, with a social development department, trying to create an instant society for the families coming up from London. They would place gates in fences of neighbouring houses, putting older folk next to young, a sort of "rent a granny" situation. These people were used to extended families. The Corporation wanted to create a community. A lot of money was spent on community projects.'*(Colin Stacey)*

Opposite, above: Here we see Danstead Way leading over the A5D and railway, with the go-kart track to the right, in the early 1980s. The environment is redolent of the 1960s dream come true. *(Colin Stacey)*

Opposite, below: Danstead Way passes Portway, shown here 20 years ago, looking towards the south-east and an abundance of drainage water, so pleasantly converted into more attractive lake land for the eye to behold and enjoy. There is no doubt of the potential of this new city environment, but, sadly, one cannot help doubting the intentions of politicians and money men. The new criteria seem to amount to 'see a space and fill it'! *(Colin Stacey)*

Not a year separates this image from the last and the space is full, yet still there is a housing crisis – strangely it is fashionable to deny this. In fact an income of almost £34,000 was needed to buy the average Milton Keynes home in August 2001 (£63,000 for the rest of Buckinghamshire, which is the most expensive part of the country to live in!) according to a National Housing Federation survey. Ray Barrowdale of the Royal Institute of Chartered Surveyors said that because Milton Keynes is a growth area it attracts people, which pushes up prices. Consequently more and more commute into work because they can't afford to live in the town. Matters aren't improving. Halifax Bank reported that the nationwide average house price in 2004 was £101,747, a 22.6 per cent increase over 2003, and house prices are 4.27 times greater than first-time buyers' salaries. In the author's opinion these are facts which comfortable people do not wish to hear or be heard! *(Colin Stacey)*

The town centre viewed from the National Bowl, 15 April 1983. The Bowl is now a world-famous concert venue but with a history rooted in the region's past, deriving its shape from its origins as a clay pit for brick-working. *(Colin Stacey)*

Early days for Furzton Lake, at Coldharbour Pit, looking from Chaffron Way in the early 1980s. This is a most welcome leisure area today. *(Colin Stacey)*

Opposite, above: The outlook is stark in this early 1980s winter view of Fulmer Street (Grid Road V3), with Blackmoor Gate leading off to the right and pleasant-sounding Emerson Valley falling away to the left. These are rich pastures for the developers, offering a seemingly workable blend of town and country life. *(Colin Stacey)*

Opposite, below: Looking at Fulmer Street today, the extent of new housing development in this western part of Milton Keynes near Bletchley is evident. It is a fast road and a nerve-racking place for an errant photographer. I was particularly amazed by the speed of a passing dustcart, but the regime of target-setting prevalent in privatised services combined with the numbers of parked cars creates a need to hurry to keep up. *(Robert Cook)*

Above: The town limits, Tattenhoe Street, 1983. The only flies in the ointment here are national grid power lines, which have been linked to leukaemia through the effects of high electromagnetic fields. An artist recently demonstrated how an array of fluorescent tubes placed under power lines picks up sufficient energy to glow significantly. We may ask what these energy flows do to people living in houses underneath but Milton Keynes, like the rest of energy-mad Britain, needs a lot of current, whatever the price. *(Colin Stacey)*

Opposite, above: Development has reached the western border with Buckinghamshire in this Tattenhoe scene from May 1997. Workmen told the author that they had uncovered religious artefacts. As the town runs out of room it will soon be knocking on Buckinghamshire County's door. *(Robert Cook)*

Opposite, below: The same area today shows that take-up for a proposed industrial site has been slower than hoped. The slowness of Milton Keynes to fulfil its original plan has been blamed by some on the winding-up of the Development Corporation and on Buckinghamshire County Council running things down ready for the unitary authority. Some see this as a sign that Prescott's new grand plans could flounder. Meanwhile soil is heaped across the roadway to keep out gypsies who favour this country location for their huge encampments. *(Robert Cook)*

Snelshall Street (V1), linking Buckinghamshire with the new town, pictured in March 2000, before the duelling that has turned this section into a race track before traffic reaches the still-winding section of the A421 into Buckingham, to the M40 and A34 and commutervilles everywhere. Buckinghamshire was where the dream started with county architect Fred Pooley back in 1964, when he planned a 23,000-acre town for 250,000 residents, complete with monorail, having foreseen the future horrors of car congestion and road carnage. Alas, he was almost alone in a world of hard-faced businessmen and expedient politicians. It is notable that as yet there is still only one employer based on this site but housing is steadily advancing over the hillside from the direction of Westcroft. (Robert Cook)

3

Old Ways

Bottle Dump corner on the A421, August 1992. The author learned to ride a bike on this road when it was still only a B-road, a country lane. Now long-term plans envisage it as a dual carriageway into Buckinghamshire and beyond. Phase one of the project is to bypass the sharp right-hander by the historic salvage works. New town limits are denoted by the tall lamp standards in the near distance. This is where the old and new meet, temporarily, before the old is overlain. Modern traffic needs modern roads, though being Britain the planners will never keep pace with the cars. At the second preliminary enquiry into Milton Keynes expansion in Northampton, the Highways Agency representative stated that he would not be able to meet the March submission deadline and that his report would only be a strategic view, not capable of pinpointing hot spots of overload resulting from the new 30-year expansion proposals. Meanwhile Milton Keynes environment director Brian Sandom reported to the transport committee that the road network was not likely to achieve acceptable standards (at current budget levels) and was expected to decline. Cabinet transport boss Graham Mabbutt said in January 2004 that there was an extra £200,000 for the following year, but this would only cover inflation and was nowhere near enough, although it was as much as the council could provide given its financial situation. He admitted an extra £1 million a year was needed to get roads up to scratch. *(Robert Cook)*

The A421 viewed from Bottle Dump roundabout during road improvements that merged the route with the city system in July 1992. *(Robert Cook)*

This photograph, taken from approximately the same location in May 1999, shows the old road incorporated into the Redway system, with height barriers and substantial bollards designed to keep out travelling people and gypsies who have camped in the area and, as in so many amenity areas, despoiled the site with waste and scrap metal. *(Robert Cook)*

This is the junction of the old Roman Watling Street with Bletchley's overspill estate link road, Whaddon Way. The historic route encouraged settlement in the area and was mimicked in the 1950s by almost parallel routing of the M1. Nowadays Watling Street's burden is relieved by the A5D. Pictured in 1983, it no longer provides a speedy cut through to the A421. *(Colin Stacey)*

The old Groveway bridge under the railway, late 1970s. Groveway has been renowned as the home of greyhound and speedway racing locally. Despite so much large-scale modern development this area remains much as it used to be. *(Colin Stacey)*

The entrance to Shenley Lodge and the now defunct wind generator at the energy-efficient housing development. Margaret Thatcher lavished praise on the idea when she visited the Energy World Exhibition, but the generator was switched off because some residents did not like the noise. The device has now been removed. *(Colin Stacey)*

Opposite, above: Heading out of Bletchley on Watling Street soon leads us to Cowley & Wilson's Vauxhall dealership at Great Holm, seen here, looking to the south-west, *c.* 1979. *(Colin Stacey)*

Opposite, below: By the 1980s car sales were big business and the old place was receiving a facelift. It has had a few more since then and is now part of the big Lex Vauxhall dealership. The author recalls a stint working there as a car valet, struggling to keep washing and vacuuming up to speed with the service centre output. *(Robert Cook)*

Back on the south side of the old road in 1983, we see here the closed-off former road from Watling Street into Shenley. Much development is afoot. *(Colin Stacey)*

Opposite, above: The Energy World exhibition at Shenley, 1988. *(Colin Stacey)*

Opposite, below: Still plenty of green landscape up for grabs here at Knowlehill on the northern side of Watling Street. Knowlehill is the setting for the pretty teardrop lakes. *(Colin Stacey)*

Stony Stratford town centre, *c.* 1980. Though Lord Campbell back in the 1960s exhorted all in the designated new city area to view themselves as Milton Keynesians, Stony Stratford retains a sense of its historic identity. In this scene the good old Bletchley & District Co-op was still present in traditional guise. *(Colin Stacey)*

Opposite, above: The Shenley–Loughton Road which crosses the A5, early 1980s; the site for Shenley Church Inn is being prepared on the left. This old village with its Church End and Brook End was going to experience big changes as a result of the grand plan. The church, just in view, top right, has stones built into it by monks who came when William Rufus was king. *(Colin Stacey)*

Opposite, below: Only the road and the church on the horizon, where the rector lived in his Georgian mansion, and the line of the road, informs us that this modern estate has any connection with the picture above. The road has been incorporated into the estate and a large modern inn is just out of view, left. *(Robert Cook)*

A short journey north takes us to the nineteenth-century railway town of Wolverton, its industrial history still evident from the neat straight lines of former LMS railway works housing. There is little of the old ways about the place now. This splendid old fire station, seen here in about 1979, had to make way for a Tesco store. *(Colin Stacey)*

The LMS railway transformed this village of Saxon origins into a lively town – and then came Milton Keynes. Bob Maxwell MP had favoured twin cities of Bletchley and Milton Keynes. He was ignored, and like Bletchley Wolverton has been rather sidelined. This image shows demolition of the old railway station under way in the 1980s. Only a rump remains of the once great railway engineering works, though there is new business maintaining the Pendolino tilting trains. How sad, though, that the British-invented tilting train had to be manufactured abroad and imported; the potential skill of British youth lacks the opportunities of generations gone by. *(Colin Stacey)*

A closer view of the flimsy old Wolverton station structure, crumbling under the might of modern machinery. These are the 1980s, when state-owned industries had to become leaner and fitter in preparation for inevitable privatisation. Curiously, a leading Tory figure has admitted that they may have got privatisation wrong. Not often does a politician of any party admit even to the possibility of making a mistake, let alone that a mistake has actually been made. Thus, if expansion plans for Milton Keynes are as half-baked as they appear to some of us, it will take a long time and a lot of misery before anyone might come close to admitting it. (*Colin Stacey*)

The Redway, leading across the railway bridge into Blue Bridge estate, Wolverton, *c.* 1980. (*Colin Stacey*)

Miller's Way Bridge under construction along Blue Bridge Redway in Wolverton. *(Colin Stacey)*

North Buckinghamshire Sports Hall, looking as if it is in the way of the emerging Stonebridge roundabout, in the early 1980s. *(Colin Stacey)*

A virginal Stonebridge roundabout viewed in the early 1980s when Britain seemed to be entering a new golden age of freedom, particularly for motorists. This pretty view reminds us that North Buckinghamshire countryside may not be outstanding but does contain some definite beauty. Ouse Valley Park, South Northamptonshire and Newport Pagnell are not far in the distance, with good old Wolverton behind the cameraman. This view shows us something of the city's Redways which have less of their planned shrubbery owing to problems with muggers and sex offenders on the prowl for fresh-air-loving victims. *(Colin Stacey)*

From the map Stony Stratford looks like a promontory on an island's western coast. The place juts out as if it belongs elsewhere. It has too much history to become a forgotten part of a larger whole. Not far beyond is the road to Old Stratford and another county. This is the old **Stratford A5 and Deanshanger** Road in 1978, with not a car in sight. *(Colin Stacey)*

If Milton Keynes was going to be the boom town envisaged, then people and their goods would have to have more road space in and out, not just within. This early 1980s picture shows work under way at the junction of Old Stratford Road with the Buckingham–Northampton road, with earthworks in place for a large roundabout, awaiting an intended new carriageway demarcated by wooden fencing. *(Colin Stacey)*

Within a few months significant changes have taken place that forewarn of today's whirling traffic way, and consequently traffic lights are now busily in operation. *(Colin Stacey)*

This quiet spot on the A422 Buckingham–Northampton road west of Milton Keynes near Old Stratford had changed very little for decades when this shot was taken in the late 1970s. (*Colin Stacey*)

A short time later this had all changed because of the traffic flow anticipated from the knock-on effects of expanding Milton Keynes and its near neighbour Northampton. (*Colin Stacey*)

The old road from Stony Stratford to Deanshanger, with preparation of a new road under way, 1980. Deanshanger is one of many natural dormitory villages for the new metropolis, and this creates huge demands upon local roads for miles around. As the expansion planners have recognised, the impact of so much additional housing will have to be shared by neighbouring authorities. *(Colin Stacey)*

The modern road from Stony Stratford to Deanshanger is traversed by the cycle way bridge, in keeping with the city's environmental enthusiasm for the bicycle. *(Robert Cook)*

4

AD – After Development

What better way to follow up development, obviously, than with more development. However, the 1990s brought a short breathing space, more because of the economic incompetence of John Major's governments than because of planning. The new city, which had struggled to get off the ground owing to the parsimony and lack of vision of previous governments, struggled to fulfil its 30-year plan and still has not done so. This picture shows a band playing in front of a sign proudly announcing 'New Toilets' in Central Milton Keynes Shopping Centre, December 1999. Judging by the lady pictured on the far right, the budget even seems to run to employing a cleaner!

Bletchley man Eddy Hancock fired the last steam engine on the Oxford–Cambridge line and has seen many changes hereabouts. Of Milton Keynes' expansion plans he remarked, 'I expect the idea is great but it's a city in a wilderness. I don't know what it's like at night as I don't go over there. The public transport is appalling. Problems on the estates are what people have made them. Being an old Bletchley man I preferred it as it was. I don't look forward to it getting any bigger. It's expanded Bletchley but the facilities are worse. There used to be three public toilets, now there's only one.' *(Robert Cook)*

The adverse effect of Milton Keynes on trees has been twofold. British rulers love red tape and paperwork. Thirty years of Milton Keynes Mark I used a great deal. Milton Keynes Mark II has got off to a good start by requiring forty copies of each submission from interested parties to April 2004's Enquiry in Public. The second effect has been the sheer number chopped down to make way for the city, probably enough for the paperwork. The planned tree-plantings around new development are threatened by health and safety legislation, and the fact that marauders use them as cover for Redway crimes. However, not all trees are caught in the path of progress. The best example of preservation must be the Old Oak in Midsummer Place (see *Milton Keynes in the News*, Cook & Shouler). Here is another in Bond Avenue, Bletchley, near the Gazette offices. As these before-and-after pictures from around 1979 reveal, some trees gained a more attractive setting from development. *(Colin Stacey)*

During the 1980s, when lovers of the countryside might have thought it was time to stop the city growing, even more houses were being constructed, with roads and walkways to connect them, like this new Redway over Danstead Way. *(Colin Stacey)*

Milton Keynes is renowned for its diverse architecture. Brian O'Sullivan, Clerk of Works, recalled a couple of trendy young architects working for the Development Corporation in the early days who had modern ideas and great influence. Their trendiness earned them the nickname 'the pop group'. Here is a fine example of ground-breaking design along the A5, the Netto supermarket under construction. It was recently badly damaged by fire. *(Colin Stacey)*

An immaculately turned-out United Counties Bristol Lodekka in a very tidy Bletchley Road (Queensway West), in April 1969. The United Counties and Road Tram Car Company started life as a private company after acquiring the assets of the Wellingborough Motor Omnibus Company on 1 September 1921, including thirty-seven vehicles. It became the United Counties Omnibus Company in 1933 after the Tilling Group takeover. Tillings used buses built by their Bristol subsidiary, taking over local bus services in 1952. (*Andrew Shouler*)

Tillings was nationalised by a postwar Labour government seeking a coordinated transport system. Against the odds the National Bus Company, of which United Counties was a well-run part with local depots in Bletchley and Stony Stratford, survived until the mid-1980s, when the Thatcher government organised a cut-price sale of state assets, including United Counties. The aim was to promote competition and end subsidies. This was an awkward situation for Milton Keynes bus services because it was never designed for convenient or manageable routes. The rump of United Counties went to Stagecoach East, leaving Milton Keynes served by various successors and facing an uncertain public transport future. This image shows the final days of the old company in 1980, with a Bristol VRT III sporting both National Bus and City Bus logos along with United Counties. (*Andrew Shouler*)

Milton Keynes gained a showcase railway station in 1982, opened by Prince Charles on 14 May, next to a grand, marble-clad bus station. The latter is now declared surplus to requirements because too few buses and coaches use it, and national train services are regularly berated. With all the foresight one expects of British politicians, Barbara Castle closed down Oxford–Cambridge passenger services in 1967. Winslow, destined to be a Milton Keynes dormitory and eventual suburb, watched its station collapse, eventually demolished for more houses. There are no definite plans to reopen this vital east–west route through Milton Keynes. This image shows the royal train passing through the derelict station in 1983. A new site is earmarked for a Winslow Halt should the line reopen, but with a meagre sixteen parking places and in the midst of another planned housing development. (James McLernon)

This is the old iron bridge over the Oxford–Cambridge line at Winslow, September 2002, a site destined to be neighbour to 250 new homes. Winslow offers little excitement for young people. The average age is 39, and 25 per cent of the population are children. Local politicians are not exactly on the wavelength of youth. This young lady is telling a Central Television news crew why she wants to see train services reinstated to Milton Keynes, because there are lots of shops and good night life. City life is something else when you are young. Perceptions vary, and so does need – you can't please everyone. (Robert Cook)

Manufacturing is rare in modern Milton Keynes but veteran entrepreneur Jim Marshall has been making a go of it locally since the 1960s. His name is a byword for excellence in the music industry. These girls are hard at work building his world-famous amplifiers at the Denbigh factory and company headquarters.

Opposite, above: Some grumbled at the plan to extend a shopping centre that already seemed vast. Ray Bellchambers of the original Development Corporation had written to a local paper protesting at plans to extend Marks & Spencer on to the city square in front of the Church of Christ the Cornerstone. Then came Midsummer Place and a threat to a fine old oak tree. Was nothing sacred in the face of development? Here we see early days at the Midsummer extension in September 1998; the dome of the church, like a mini St Paul's, is just visible. *(Robert Cook)*

Opposite, below: Critics of Milton Keynes' expansion argue that it is far too service- and retail-dependent in job terms and that if consumers turned away from credit the town's problems would worsen. Rents are high in the central shopping centre. This picture shows the last weeks of C&A in December 2000. The Europe-based company could not make a profit in the highly competitive and fickle fashion market. A company's collapse when it comes can be swift as a former Scott meatworker recalled: 'I went off on holiday. When I came back on the night shift two weeks later, a mate said, "Jim, have you found another job yet?" I didn't know what he was talking about. Then he told me the place was closing in two weeks. I came to Bletchley from the navy in the 1960s. Dyson's die castings was run by an ex-naval officer. He organised it so that we came out of the service and straight into a job. Bletchley was different then.' *(Robert Cook)*

Newton Road, Newton Longville, August 1993: one of the large waste-container vehicles rumbles away from the former Bletchley brickworks and into the village. The old brick pits have found new life as rubbish tips and tippers thunder through the old village from miles around. Anxieties reached fever pitch following a large incinerator scheme which, in the words of Milton Keynes Friends of the Earth spokesman Andrew Lockley, 'is so expensive to build that it becomes a big hungry monster, emissions can be quite horrible and the single greatest source of nitrous oxide. Our campaign was an example of people power in Milton Keynes, the capital of apathy. We got the scheme modified. Incinerator technology has improved.' *(Robert Cook)*

Blue Lagoon, Bletchley, July 1998. This former brick pit, or knot hole as it is known in the industry, is the focal point of a nature park near the Lakes estate, Water Eaton. Before Milton Keynes such abandonment was usual but, given the huge market for waste, there was even talk of opening the area up to waste disposal vehicles in 2003, and building a dedicated road through. *(Robert Cook)*

Public utilities were part of the big Tory sell-off and this is all that is left of East Midlands Electricity's big maintenance facility in Wolverton in November 2003; the site is now up for redevelopment. Business is now controlled from Castle Donington, miles away with only minimal staff and facilities locally. The author had first-hand experience of the streamlined set-up in October 2002; storms brought down a tree across power cables leaving him without power for nine days before Castle Donington could find the time and resources to make repairs. He experienced nine more power failures over the next twelve months before a reliable power supply was established. Nationally, we are told that we must expect such difficulties in future, such is the balance between supply and demand for this vital product. Why don't they have that problem in France? *(Robert Cook)*

Meanwhile as town growth approached fulfilment of the original 30-year plan, redevelopment and infilling proceeded apace in sought after areas, like Bletchley. This garage site on the Whaddon Way–Buckingham Road junction was cleared in December 2000 for the construction of Buckingham Court 1/2-bedroom apartments. Older council properties are temporarily opened up to give us a view of older ideals in mass housing. *(Robert Cook)*

Meanwhile, in the heart of old Bletchley, once-spacious gardens where old railwaymen would have grown a few vegetables and chatted over the garden fence have become like gold dust, ripe for highly profitable infilling during the 1980s. These two photographs were taken only months apart. *(Colin Stacey)*

In the meantime Milton Keynes has pulled trade away from Bletchley town centre exactly as people like Bob Maxwell MP had feared. There are plans in the air for revamping the once diverse and popular Bletchley shopping centre which has grown tattier by the year since 1979, with a plethora of charity shops. The industry has become so prolific here that it has even reached superstore level. This was Cambridge Street in June 1999, and the theme was 'Care Albania'. *(Robert Cook)*

It is sometimes easier to feel pain for folk far away and write of a street beggar's plight as being due to laziness. Here is Graham begging outside the Point Cinema in 2001. A *Citizen* news report on 27 November 2002 called for urgent investigation into the lack of affordable housing. Over 1,400 people were living in temporary accommodation, and many under-25s were forced to move out because of soaring prices. Labour leader Nigel Long wanted to know why the planning system could not provide more affordable housing. Cabinet member Irene Henderson said the council was doing all it could to cope with increasing demand but it was like trying to put a quart into a pint pot. *(Robert Cook)*

Who cares about homelessness when you have football? The town teems with Sunday morning child and youth teams, and the author knows that furious rivalry is as common among watching parents as it is on the field. After initial FA opposition Wimbledon Dons have moved to Milton Keynes, and the town has high hopes of a new stadium at Denbigh for which planning has been approved. In the meantime they must make do with the converted National Hockey Centre, seen here near completion in 1995. New owner Pete Winkleman has his work cut out after a recent 5–0 thrashing from a side including five players sold to raise cash. Locals are hoping for a return to the glory days of 1988 when the Dons walked away with the FA cup. *(Robert Cook)*

But for real escapism try Star Wars. Here is baddie-made-good Darth Vader, actor David Prowse, beamed into Milton Keynes Shopping Centre in December 2002 to sign autographs for fans from as far away as Portsmouth – surely another planet entirely! *(Robert Cook)*

As you might expect for a space traveller, there were other stars about when Darth Vader landed in Milton Keynes, including David Soul, alias Detective Hutchinson – though for serious escapists it is the other way around. Interestingly, David first found fame singing with a bag on his head, creating enough interest to earn him a recording contract. Then he made the mistake of taking the bag off, revealing that he was just another good-looking blond kid. Interest faded and he had to start all over again. After some shameful ventures, by his own account, he found fame difficult, got drunk and messed it up. Could there be a moral in his life story for Milton Keynes? *(Robert Cook)*

Bletchley, May 1999, and two swans have been luckier than many hopefuls, finding a home for their new family off Princes Way. But as we can see from the disintegrating multi-storey car park in the background, there is not going to be much long-term security living here! (Robert Cook)

The underside of Standing Way, viewed from a scruffy and glass-strewn footpath alongside the tracks. The graffiti on the bridge show how easy it is to vault the inadequate fence, and are evidence of poor track security. Anything more substantial would cost money, however, and when this photograph was taken in March 2000 Railtrack were still looking for profits to please hungry directors and shareholders. Such views from the underside are not popular when leaders urge yet more growth, crying out success even when things go wrong. *(Robert Cook)*

Gypsies are among those eager to share in the Milton Keynes 'success story'. Their leaders tell the press as much but many see their sizeable encampments and the mess they leave behind as something that can't be glossed over. These good people have pulled up alongside the A421 at Tattenhoe, no doubt to enjoy the rolling views and the summer air in May 1999. Sadly for them they could not camp here as yet another verge gives way to the duelling of the carriageway. *(Robert Cook)*

Oh happy days: life in Simpson, August 1995. The author first visited the village in 1971 as a young construction worker with Sidney Green Ltd, who had their compound here and brought noise and mud to a once tranquil and now much changed environment. Arthur Mee's 1920 study of Buckinghamshire described Simpson as 'another little village bordering on the meadows'. I remember those meadows, watching machines reap the last harvest of one kind of gold while our machines set seeds for another kind, ripping through the countryside at an amazing rate. But as Baden Powell, pictured here at his front gate with Muriel Cousins in 1994, said, after a long and happy life, 'the secret is a contented mind'. *(Robert Cook)*

The railway line from Newport Pagnell to Wolverton was another victim of enthusiasm for the motor car. Here is a relic at Newport Pagnell of that other world, that different time: the old signal post for 'Nobby Newport' as the engine was called, photographed in the 1980s when development had changed so many old places almost beyond recognition. *(Colin Stacey)*

5

Wild West

Outside Central Milton Keynes railway station, October 2003. Milton Keynes has been a Labour stronghold ever since boundaries were re-drawn cancelling out rural Tory influence, and it is surprising to see protests against the party messiah Tony Blair. Although many socialists believe that Blair has betrayed the party and is in hock to global capitalism, which is about endless growth and ruining the planet, few hurrying commuters stopped to read the messages 'Blair Must Go' and 'Out of Iraq Now'.

However, there is local anger now as government rushes to impose its plan for doubling the size of Milton Keynes over an area of 18,000 hectares using, as Colin Fox of the Economic Partnership overseeing development put it, 'the engine of the local economy' to sustain it. He added that Milton Keynes could deliver, had the track record, and that there was a need for more houses. There is very little detail about how exactly government will fund expansion. The bulk of the expansion is to be in the west, along with significant redevelopment of Bletchley to reverse its decline. *(Robert Cook)*

Queensway, Bletchley, named following the Queen's visit in 1965 but definitely not fit for a king or queen nowadays. There was once a press photo of our monarch pausing in a McDonald's drive-through, but it is hard to imagine her eating here – no disrespect! But maybe she will one day because there is a brand new scheme to completely rebuild the Bletchley centre, relocating the leisure centre and redeveloping the site for 400 homes, plus conversion of Stephenson House into apartments with beautified surroundings, and Princes Way will be realigned – with homes along its entire length. *(Robert Cook)*

Opposite, above: John Prescott stalking through Milton Keynes Shopping Centre on the election campaign leading to his party's landslide victory in 1997, when the author heard the now deputy prime minister say, 'Things have to change.' Who says politicians never keep their promises, just so long as they are vague enough? Wearing his environmental hat, his has been the name most associated with the Milton Keynes & South-East Regional Strategy. *(Ken Gorman)*

Opposite, below: The basic problem with the current expansion plan is that it is about encouraging more people to move in, not to add resources and homes to meet existing demand or to complete the original plan. The lack of resources has an effect on educational provision. Discipline is a challenge, as Despina Pavlou, headteacher of Lord Grey School, knows. Following a fire and a pupil's exclusion the authority faces a £10,000 damages claim from the aggrieved ex-pupil. Schools are struggling and the education department reported a £650,000 overspend in November 2003, leading to a series of freezes and cuts. Some parents have been criticised for sending children to schools in neighbouring counties like the Royal Latin Grammar school in Buckinghamshire, but Milton Keynes schools are in the modern huge GCSE factory pattern. This low-lying creation off Chaffron Way and Tattenhoe is undergoing extension to accommodate vastly increasing rolls in January 2001. *(Robert Cook)*

This picture, taken in August 1987, shows the idyllic country town of Winslow, 10 miles west of Milton Keynes and too close for the comfort of some. Great and Little Horwood are on the horizon and there have already been plans to fill in the fields between (formerly a wartime aerodrome and therefore nice and level) to make one big place that could so easily connect up with Whaddon and the town. Such a view, though much more thoughtful in its detail, has been envisaged by Milton Keynes west expansion planning consultant David Lock. Indeed David's plan to include a grand park around Whaddon Hall, with transit corridors for frequent trams and restored Oxford–Cambridge rail services might be ideal. But this is 2004 and the planning and inclination to spend is nothing like that of the even poorer 1960s – so much for Britain being the world's fourth largest economy! As a fellow attendee at the second preliminary enquiry into Milton Keynes expansion observed in February 2004, there is no grand overview for the next 30 years, only bite-size chunks. *(Robert Cook)*

Opposite, top: In the original plan it was manifest that the new town would provide mainly for London overspill and jobs. The executive class would be more able to afford homes in surrounding countryside. This July 2001 view of the western expansion zone of Milton Keynes gives a clue as to how nice it is out there, so it is not surprising that country folk old and new may be somewhat alarmed by urban expansion, especially now John Prescott has raised minimum dwelling densities to 40 per acre. But how else can anything affordable for the housing backlog and poorer incomers be made available and how can such settlements be comfortable neighbours with more extravagant properties? *(Robert Cook)*

Opposite, centre: Preparing the ground in May 1997 for the great way west: we see here road improvements, near Whaddon on the A421 Milton Keynes–Buckingham road. The surface in use is temporary while material extracted from the Finmere bypass west of Buckingham is used to level out a big dip in the old road, far right – a notorious black spot on a route that has become a commuter and motorbike race track. *(Robert Cook)*

Opposite, bottom: Warren Farm, Little Horwood, just off the A421: the developer's sign is up, and Milton Keynes Real Estate are converting the old buildings into apartments. Work is due for completion in October 2004, with plans to convert the old granary modified because of asbestos content. This was originally a pig farm but is worth millions for development. It is not surprising so many farmers are giving up the land when they are up against punitive government policies. Development will create ten flats and two houses aimed at the executive market, with no new build. The company are also set to develop in Mursley, aiming to provide some affordable housing. Milton Keynes is closing in on leafy Buckinghamshire. The land opposite Warren Farm would make an ideal golf course. *(Robert Cook)*

Sheep Street, Winslow, winter 2000: traffic queues up into the High Street bottleneck during the commuter rush hour. House prices in Winslow have rocketed owing to its proximity to Milton Keynes, with younger and poorer folks fighting for what's left of council housing. Car owners abound and must show off their status symbols; juggernauts must thunder by to feed the consumer society. Another 250 houses are planned for the other side of town, generating at least another 500 cars. A relief road promised in 1931 has been cancelled because housing was built along the planned route in the 1960s and 1970s, without any thought being given toward future congestion. So why should we trust the planners now? *(Robert Cook)*

Opposite: Autumn 2002 is here and Winslow's county councillor David Rowlands, standing on the old Iron Bridge over the railway, informs Central TV news that signals were up for a new Winslow station. The old railway line still has not been reopened and the second preliminary Milton Keynes expansion enquiry heard that it was not imminent. However, Cllr Rowlands took issue with Cllr Robert Cook's pessimism about the line at a meeting to discuss putting 250 houses in the fields visible just beyond the bridge, and announced yet another study at a cost of £3 million. Why don't they just get on with rebuilding the line which was so vital to Milton Keynes in the first place and is vital now if expansion is to get off to a proper start? If they want the case elaborated any more painfully than that I will do so for just £1 million! *(Robert Cook)*

Tony Sofair chairs a meeting of North Buckinghamshire Parishes Consortium at Winslow Town Council Chamber in February 2004. Tony was a member of the original Stake Holders meetings, dealing with the implications of the Roger Timms enquiry which started the Milton Keynes expansion ball rolling.

Easily vulnerable to accusations of nimbyism, condemned out of hand for having large comfortable homes in rich ghettos, residents of these parishes are naturally concerned about the effects of new city expansion on the rural environment. In summary, they recognise that they love the countryside in which they choose to live, arguing that city expansion will not provide newcomers with a rural way of life – so why not direct overspill population to existing urban areas like Birmingham and Coventry that are crying out for development? Meanwhile, the government must respond to their advisers' calculations that 4 million new homes will be needed by 2022, and that while 70 per cent of new housing demand is in London and the south, only 50 per cent of new building is in that region. The government defends itself against accusations of swallowing up 18,000 hectares of green field, boasting that with higher housing densities they can create desirable homes just as eighteenth-century developers did in London, Bath and Edinburgh. But while the enquiry spends much time working out how quickly the houses can be built, questions of improving existing infrastructure and the manner and schedule of providing additional infrastructure are hardly considered; the enquiry simply pushes key questions into the future. (*Robert Cook*)

Town planner David Lock of David Lock Associates studies two major plans for what is mainly the western expansion of Milton Keynes. On the left is the official Milton Keynes Strategic Vision, on the right is his firm's 'Strategic Overview of the West of Milton Keynes, A Sustainable Western Expansion' (pages 38–41). The two are significantly different, the latter extending right out to Winslow in a planned way, with a huge park at the centre in Whaddon Chase, the hunting ground of rich overlords well into the twentieth century. Instead of vague terms like 'Potential Trans-City Rapid Transit Routes', and the total vagueness of making it up as time passes and as the sprawl and traffic jams reach Winslow, he allows for space and civilised, workable transport means and corridors. Most villages would remain outside the boundary, but traffic and light pollution would be a constant reminder that city life was near. There would still be conflict. As it stands there is a plan, most likely to be approved, offering creeping development into the west and significant traffic impact in the near future. All the signs, from the second preliminary enquiry attended by the author, were that road and rail improvements will lag. The meeting heard that the Highways Agency reported that they could not be precise about traffic impact or hot spots and the East–West Rail representative was unable to give a detailed scheme of finance or timing for restoring the old rail link. *(Robert Cook)*

Victoria Hervey of Bedfordshire Friends of the Earth explains matters to an attendee at the second preliminary meeting for the Enquiry in Public, 17 February 2004, which evaluated the Milton Keynes and South Sub-regional Spatial Strategy. Sitting at the back in the Saints Rugby Club Conference suite I could not see, only hear the panel and the government offices man, Mr Hargreaves, and over the PA it sounded like a distant radio broadcast, fading just at the important bits and getting very loud on the trivial! However, he perked up when Milton Keynes Friends of the Earth spokesman Andrew Lockley asked, 'Would the panel go back to the drawing board if they encountered robust opposition from interested parties?' A resounding 'No!' was followed by the explanation that the plan had been decided and would be carried forward by virtue of the government's majority. People at the meeting could help them to work out the details, and the purpose of the enquiry in public was to make the plan work. Now was not the time to debate the whys and wherefores. *(Robert Cook)*

The panel at the second Preliminary Enquiry Meeting, 17 February 2004. Panel Inspector Roy Foster MA, MRTPI, is on the right, with Chairman Inspector Alan Richardson BA, MPhil, MRTPI. These are men of unquestionable qualification and integrity but can only be as good as their brief. It is not their role to question the choice of Milton Keynes or anywhere else affected by the spatial strategy. The government's representative, whose paper was only made available as we entered the meeting, made it clear that those of us being consulted were there to help make it work. When a speaker from the floor said this implied that the panel had already made up their minds, Mr Richardson answered that no one had told them what to think and that their report would be based on the enquiry's findings. The government representative replied, 'We'll then decide what to do with it.' *(Robert Cook)*

Looking south near Calverton, a scene that could be pre-war but is from the summer of 2003. This area was excluded from the original Milton Keynes but is very much in the sights of expansion proposals. Of development in this area, David Lock observes: 'The people in the rural areas are in denial of their relationship with the city, but they drive around the countryside, they live here, they work here, shop here. They have an unsustainable lifestyle. . . . The greater public good is the issue. We have a shortage of 1.8 million houses in south-east England. That is not sustainable. . . . Providing new jobs will be sustainable. . . . It is better to spend time consulting the public to get a 30-year master plan than to spend thirty years ducking and diving making it happen. . . . There is no reason why it has to go forward in bits. I am hoping that the new local development Milton Keynes partnership will commission a 30-year plan for Aylesbury, Luton and Northampton.' *(Robert Cook)*

Opposite, above: The Cock Hotel, Stony Stratford High Street, in summer 2003, and a comparison with page 12. The changes speak for themselves, but there is a high standard of conservation here. Development does not have to be destructive, 'Stony' has not lost its old world charm – yet! *(Robert Cook)*

Opposite, below: Another comparison shot, this time with page 9. It is the Green in summer 2003, a fine setting for the annual folk festival. The town supports a great tradition in folk and other acoustic music. *(Robert Cook)*

Stonhill Garage, Stewkley, December 1999. The garage has now closed and a residential conversion has been completed. Milton Keynes is not far behind this delightful old property. This doesn't worry Parish Council Chairman Arthur Lyttle who thinks the city a great success with much more potential. He says it's fulfilled the original brief, within political constraints. Some thought the shopping centre would fall into ruin. Former planning head, John Walker, ensures continuity for new development. *(Robert Cook)*

Opposite: According to the government agencies the Milton Keynes economy will sustain expansion, but the local economy is very different from the early 1960s when this picture was taken at Newton Longville brickworks; the brick kilns were turning out thousands of bricks each month and London Brick Company Limited was a cornerstone of it all. Nowadays Milton Keynes is a cross-section of the national economy with only around 17 per cent actually making anything. Milton Keynes in that sense is symbolic of the nation. Russell Hancock, far right, left all this behind shortly after this picture and a collision with a brick lorry. He and his wife emigrated to the better weather of Australia and wide open spaces. Jim and Betty Sidebottom recall a very different way of life in Newton Longville and Bletchley. Jim said: 'The village hasn't changed much since we retired to Newton Longville 21 years ago. It is already a suburb of Milton Keynes, it is so close. Being run by Milton Keynes council won't make much difference.' Jo Bromley has lived in the village for 30 years and feels the addition of 2,500 homes will destroy a rural community of 800 homes. 'Why does everywhere have to be part of an urban sprawl, why can't people have the choice? The village is already used as a cut-through by reps and lorries heading for the A5 and there will be all those houses down to the Bottle Dump roundabout.' *(Eddy Hancock)*

Shenley Church End, July 2001. This image shows us the intriguing possibilities of modern planning; like Milton Keynes village, a charming part of the past has been beautifully preserved here. Along with its near companion, Shenley Brook End, it was owned in the time of William Rufus by a monastery in Normandy, but now is the domain of wealthier locals. Milton Keynes Friends of the Earth campaigner Andrew Lockley says: 'Milton Keynes is a city of extremes. On the one hand it is one of the most soulless car-dependent places ever built. It is a city built for companies, not people. On the other hand it is an outstanding achievement of urban design, a very efficient city, very easy to use with a lot of parkland. Transport is based on the car, very efficient but not sustainable. It is deeply flawed but highly successful. The challenge is to correct what is wrong there now and build on the strengths.' *(Robert Cook)*

Central Milton Keynes undoubtedly, like many British towns, has its ugly side, but as we see here it is predominantly a glamorous place, most popular with ladies keen to keep up with the fashion scene. This is the centre in summer 2003, a cathedral of consumerism. *(Robert Cook)*

Fenny Stratford shops, 1910. These outlets served a tightly knit community but choice was limited unless you were very rich, and life was hard. Folk went to church to sing the likes of 'the rich man in his castle, the poor man at his gate, God made them high or lowly and ordered their estate'. Not many would like to go back to all those restrictions, but some locals are even worse off today and it is going to be difficult if not impossible to give everyone everything they need and want. *(Colin Scott)*

There is no disputing that after a shaky start Milton Keynes Shopping Centre is second to none. Rachael Webb from Stewkley says you can't beat John Lewis, but that's about all she likes. Here, playing his compositions outside that wonderful shop in December 1999, is a friend and neighbour from schooldays, John Walker. The covered square here has proved a great crowd puller with exhibitions and Christmas displays. *(Robert Cook)*

As Terry Wogan said when he visited in 2001, Milton Keynes is a wonderful place, for all its faults. The big question is whether it will be made better by rapid expansion. Is expanding too quickly already a reason for some of its more serious faults? None the less it is full of interesting people, like inventor and engineer Pete Sullivan who has featured on *Tomorrow's World* with his triangular caterpillar wheel for vehicles working in boggy places, like canal banks, where his own work has often taken him. More recently he hit the news with a periscope peeping out from his New Bradwell home where he had modelled his basement on a submarine. He is pictured here in 1995. *(Robert Cook)*

Whether it is a fairy tale or nightmare, we shall have to wait for the outcome, because as the government services representative told us all at the second preliminary enquiry meeting, expansion is going to happen. The government have the majority. Let's hope it is a fairy tale like this scene from Milton Keynes Carnival Parade in 2001. Of town planners, David Lock says, 'People like me become town planners out of a strong sense of vocation, we really want to make the world a better place. If you've got that fire in your belly it really makes you want to get up in the morning. Sadly an awful lot end up working for local authorities filling in forms all day long. The fire goes out.' *(Robert Cook)*

Where it all began: Buckinghamshire County Council architect Fred Pooley with a model of his original plan in 1964. At that time local MP Bob Maxwell, favouring a twin town centre approach based on Wolverton and Bletchley to ensure their prosperity and save the countryside, stated: 'From what I have been able to gather of the financial and practical feasibility of the Pooley scheme I should be surprised if the government were to decide in its favour.' In the event compulsorily purchasing open countryside in north Buckinghamshire proved cheaper than either scheme. *(Ray Bellchambers)*

And this is what it is all about for many, the finest grid road system and shopping centre in the world, seen here in the early 1990s. According to Chancellor Gordon Brown's economic forecast the country will do very well this financial year, with national growth being around 3.25 per cent. But since 1998 the nation has spent £120 billion on credit cards. Household debt, as a proportion of net income, reached 134 per cent last year against a previous peak of 112 per cent. The Bank of England has warned that the quick build-up of such debt could become unsustainable and lead to abrupt adjustment – meaning a crash. That would be very bad for a Milton Keynes already in serious financial difficulties. Brown hopes to boost the local economy and cut costs by moving civil servants to Milton Keynes, but that could add to housing pressure. He's thought of that. He wants another 120,000 houses a year on top of current proposals to flood the market and bring down prices. A key question for the expansion enquiry is: can house completions be achieved at the levels sought, bearing in mind the past performance of the housing market in this area? Unfortunately, demand outstrips supply: there are around 15,000 in temporary accommodation and you need a salary of £34,000 to be able to afford something basic. Even the Commons Select Committee says the proposals are unlikely to have any impact on reducing house prices. *(Milton Keynes in the News)*

ACKNOWLEDGEMENTS

Very many people have helped directly and indirectly with this book and each has played a vital part. Inevitably those who have guided me with other local projects have played a hidden part. Thanks must go to all those who have contributed to the photographic record – their names are with the photographs. The cooperation of the Enquiry Panel, Chairman Alan Richardson and Inspector Roy Foster was much appreciated. I am very grateful to David Lock of David Lock Associates for spending so much time talking to me about expansion and town planning matters. Martin Blane is always a guiding influence in these matters. Tony Sofair, Rachael Webb and all the members of North Buckinghamshire Parish Consortium have supplied me with considerable data. I have conducted a number of interviews of great importance to me and give great thanks to all those quoted in the text. Thanks again to Pam Essam and Colin Scott. Gratitude is due to Buckinghamshire County Council, the Campaign for the Protection of Rural England, David Rowlands, Milton Keynes Friends of the Earth, the *Milton Keynes Citizen* and *Milton Keynes News* for supplying valuable commentary over the years, Arthur Lyttle, Jo Bromley and Hermione Longton for additional research. Andrew Shouler, my co-author on a number of books, has always been able to resolve questions of detail and his perspective has informed my own over the years. I am grateful to Eddy Hancock for his wise counsel. Ray Bellchambers of the original Development Corporation set me on the road of discovery. Once again Colin Stacey has supported me with advice and through a large contribution to the photographic record and processing. If there is anything wrong with this book, it is all down to me as everyone consulted did their very best to help. Last but not least, if any credit is due to this book, some of it must go to Sutton's commissioning editor Simon Fletcher, whose idea it was in the first place.

BIBLIOGRAPHY

Robert Cook, *Bletchley Past & Present*, Sutton, 2004
Robert Cook, *Bletchley in Old Photographs*, Sutton, 1995, reprinted 2004
Robert Cook, *Bucks Bricks*, Baron Birch, 1997
Robert Cook, *Milton Keynes in Old Photographs*, Sutton, 1995
Robert Cook & Andrew Shouler, *Milton Keynes in the News*, Sutton/WHSmith, 2001
Robert Cook & Andrew Shouler, *The United Counties Story*, Tempus
A.E. Grigg, *A Job for Life*, Baron Birch, 1993